COLORING BOOKS
FOR GROWN-UPS

GRANDMA'S
QUILTS

Illustrations and book design by Cheryl Casey.
© 2015 Cheryl Casey. All rights reserved.
ISBN-13: 978-1515139133
ISBN-10: 1515139131

cherylcaseyart.com

Wingfeather Books
™
wingfeatherbooks.com

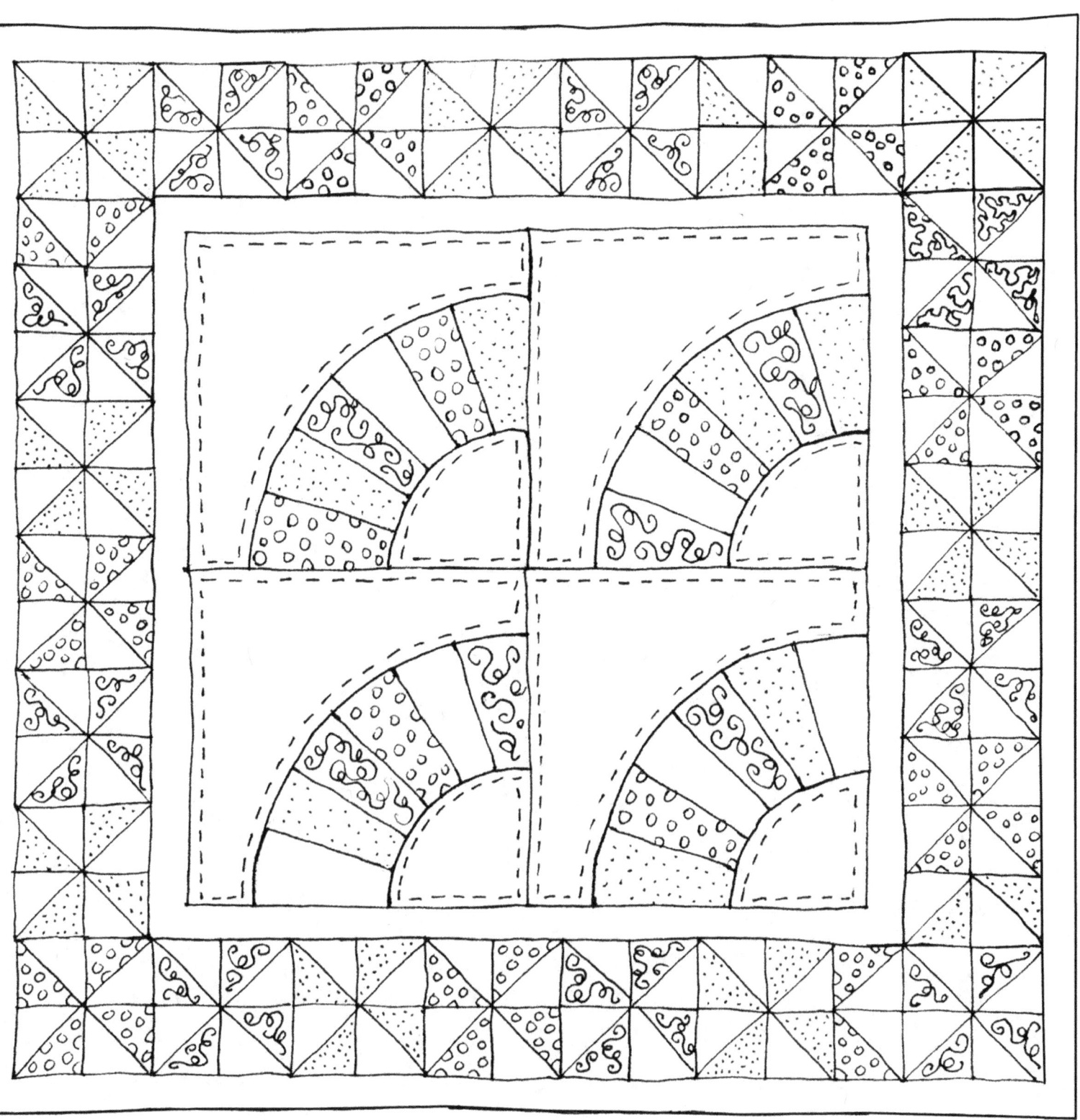

Grandmother's Fan

Snail Trails

Double Wedding Ring

Evening Star

Butterfly

Cactus Bloom

Hearts & Nine-Patches

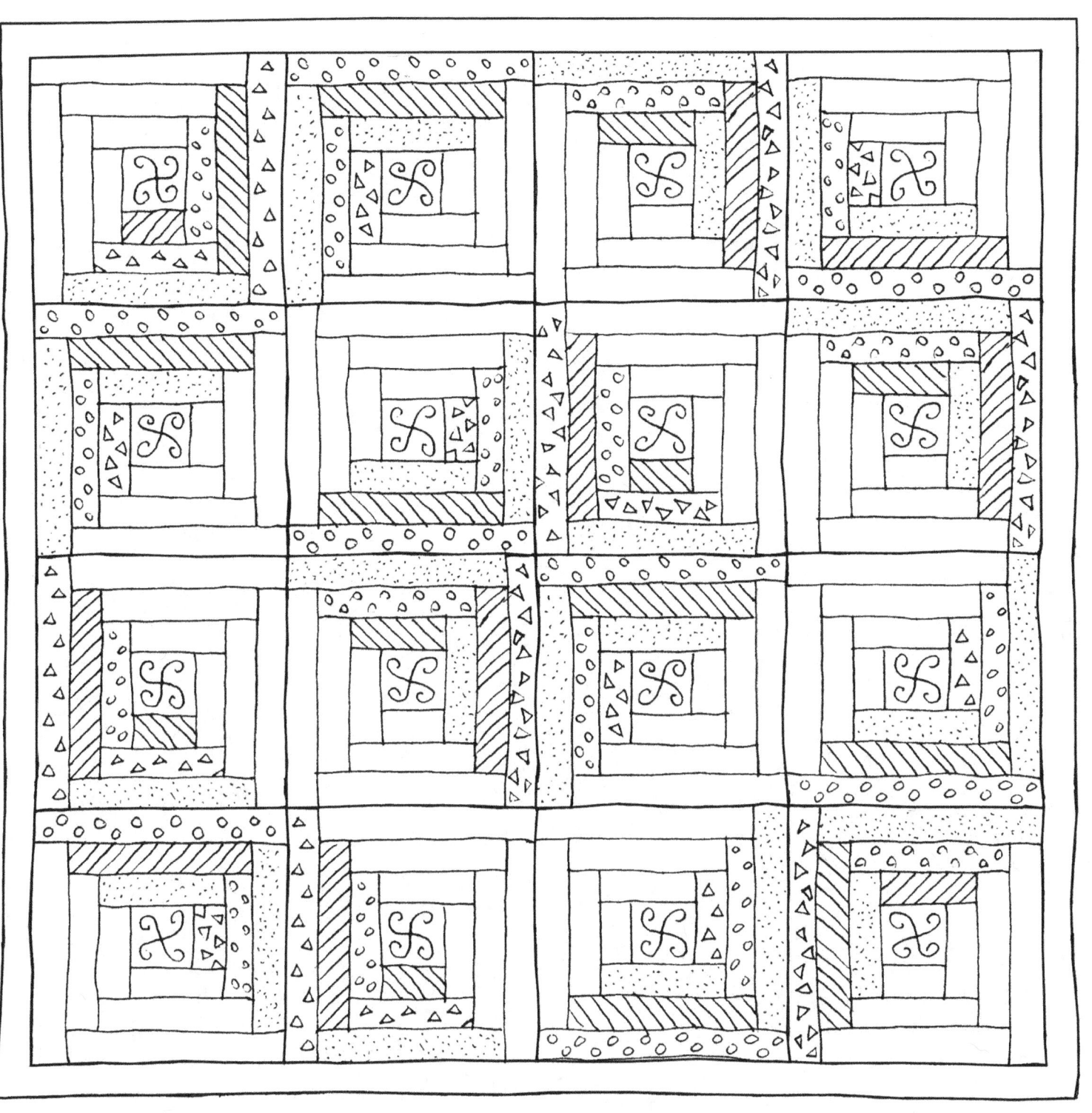

Log Cabin

Stained Glass

Eight-Point Star

Eight-Point Star Sampler

Circles

Dresden Plate Flower

Morning Star

Love

Lone Star

Dahlia

Scotty Dog

Calico Cats

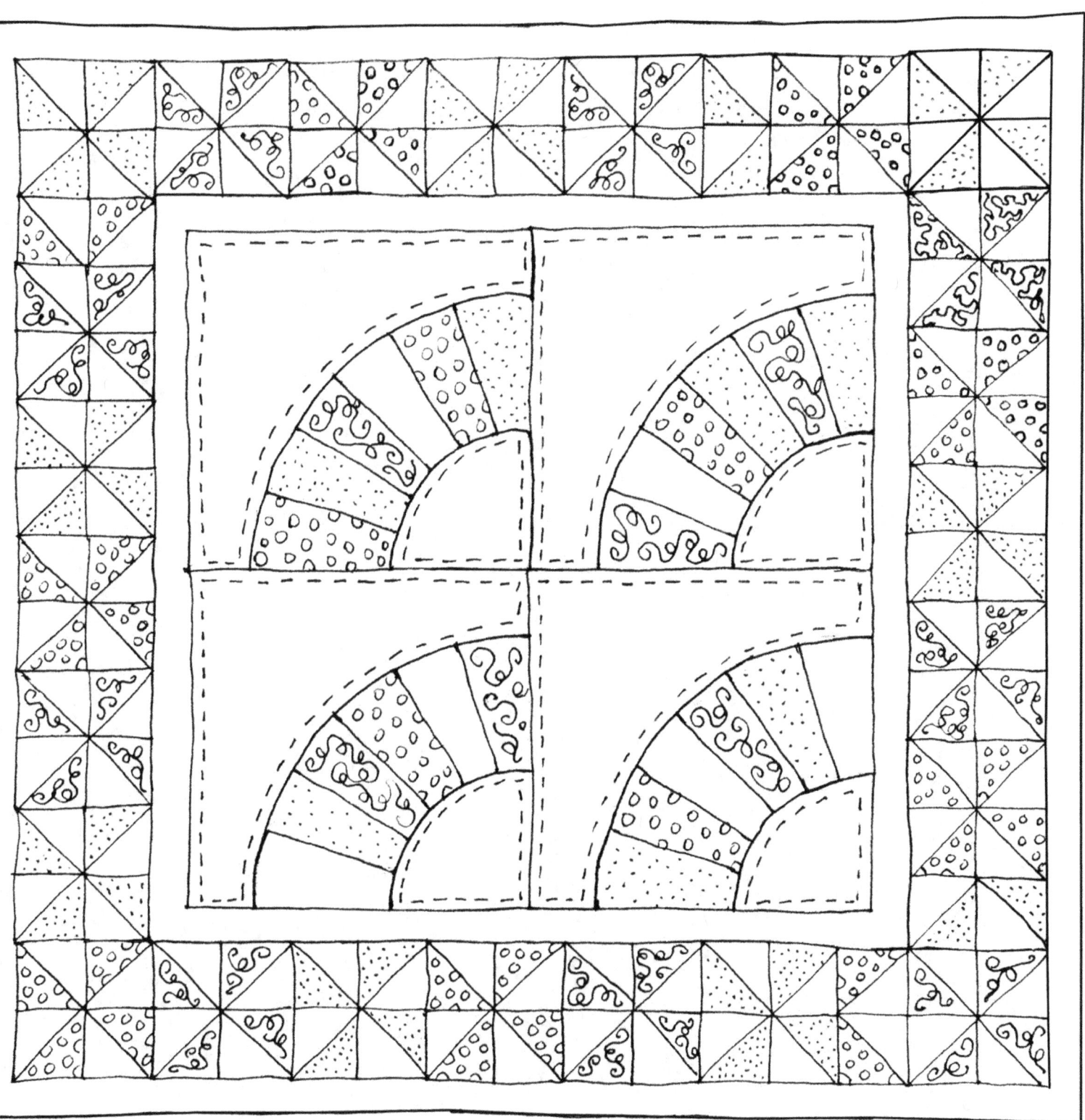

Grandmother's Fan

Snail Trails

Double Wedding Ring

Evening Star

Butterfly

Cactus Bloom

Hearts & Nine-Patches

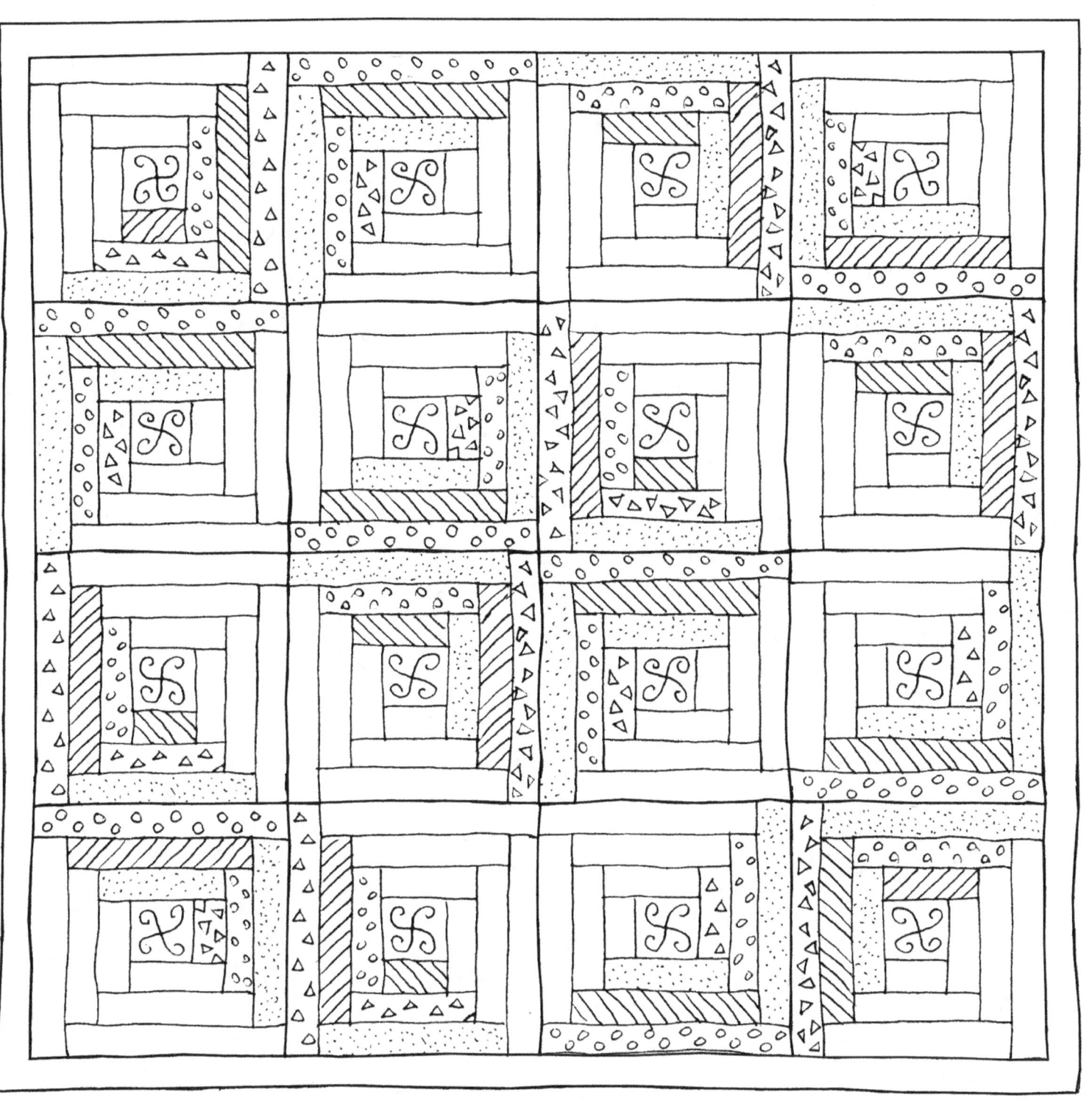

Log Cabin

Stained Glass

Eight-Point Star

Eight-Point Star Sampler

Circles

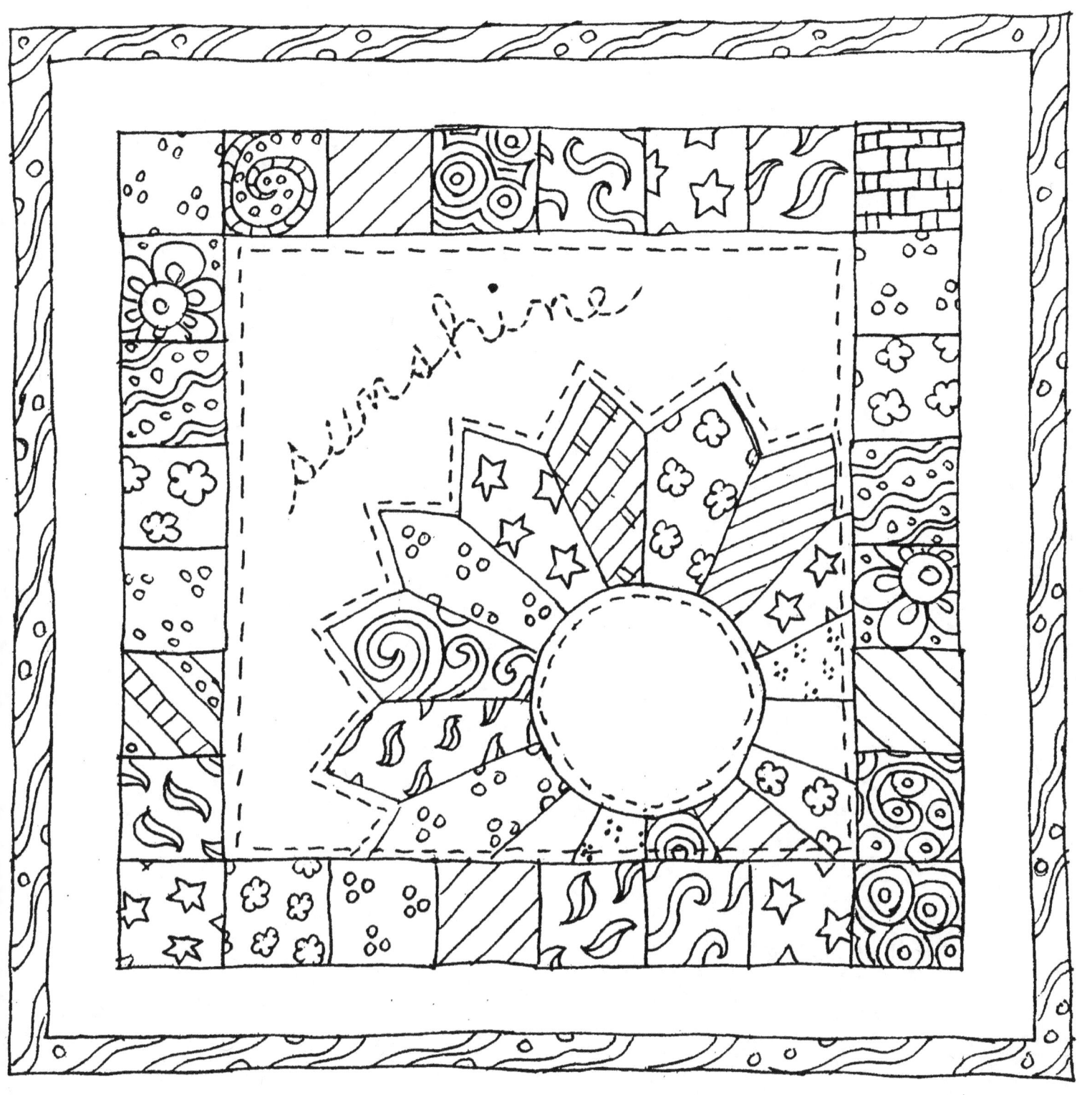

Dresden Plate Flower

Morning Star

Love

Lone Star

Dahlia

Scotty Dog

Calico Cats

BONUS coloring page from
Oodles of Doodles by Deanna Pipkin
coming September 2015
from Wingfeather Coloring Books

Tear out for blotter
paper if needed.

Tear out for blotter
paper if needed.

www.ingramcontent.com/pod-product-compliance
Lightning Source LLC
Chambersburg PA
CBHW080428290526
45791CB00008BA/2432